SPECIALLY PROTECTED AREA NO 6
Trespass or overflight prohibited by
international agreement. Area No 6
also includes any area occupied by
the rookery of Emperor penguins.

Mount Bird

Mount Erebus

Cape Royds

Barne Glacier

Cape Evans

Hut Point

Scott Base

Winter Quarters Bay

McMurdo Station

White Island

R O S S   I S L A N D

WOHLSCHLAG
BAY

LEWIS   BAY

Cape Tennyson

Wood Point

Williamson Rock
Adélie penguin rookeries

Emperor penguin rookery

Cape Crozier

WINDLESS   BIGHT

Cape MacKay

ROSS

ICE   SH

SHELF

Cape Spencer-Smith

DeepFreeze!

A Photographer's Antarctic Odyssey
in the Year 1959

Art Direction
VASSO AVRAMOPOULOU

Prints from negatives
GEORGE MARINOS

Layout
A4 ARTDESIGN

Production advisor
SUE MEDLICOTT

Printing in tritone and binding
TRIFOLIO SRL, VERONA, ITALY

Front Cover
A visitor to the McMurdo base returns to the sea ice

Back Cover
"Winter Quarters Bay", the southernmost harbor in the Southern Ocean

ISBN 978-0-9843364-0-1

INTERNATIONAL PHOTOGRAPHY PUBLISHERS LLC
Email: ippnewyork@verizon.net
Website: http://www.ippny.com

Photographer's website: http://www.mccabephotos.com

Robert A. McCabe

DeepFreeze!

A Photographer's Antarctic Odyssey
in the Year 1959

INTERNATIONAL PHOTOGRAPHY PUBLISHERS LLC

*Dedicated to the memory of the men and women
who have given their lives in the exploration
of the Antarctic continent*

ANTARCTICA is the only continent to have been discovered by the camera. Before ships entered Antarctic waters, voyages of exploration had traditionally carried expeditionary artists whose duties were to capture, in watercolors and sketches, the novel landscapes, wildlife and native peoples they encountered. Early expeditions to the Great White South, on the other hand, were accompanied by the camera. The first photographs of the Antarctic were taken in 1897, by the American Frederick Cook (later of North Pole and Mount McKinley notoriety), while serving as ship's surgeon on the Belgica. When the ship became trapped in ice and her crew inadvertently became the first men to endure an Antarctic winter, Cook turned his camera to making portraits of the beleaguered ship and men as well as "scientific" studies of ice and wildlife.

In these earliest Antarctic ventures, the camera functioned principally as an extension of the artist's sketchbook. But when Robert Falcon Scott sailed south in 1910 on the Terra Nova, the camera and photographer played a more self-conscious and professional role. Aware that the drama of an expedition could be captured, and commercially exploited, by still and moving film, expedition photographer Herbert Ponting embarked upon what would now be recognized as documentary filmmaking, as well as consciously artistic endeavors. Through his lenses, even in black and white, Antarctica's landscape shimmers and broods in dramatic ends-of-the-earth light and shadows. The art of icescape photography was later perfected by Australian Frank Hurley in his brilliant series of photographs chronicling, and dramatically elevating, the ordeal of Sir Ernest Shackleton's 1914-1916 Endurance expedition.

Robert A. McCabe's *DeepFreeze!*, therefore, not only chronicles what was itself an historic venture – "A Photographer's Antarctic Odyssey in the Year 1959" in the words of the book's subtitle – but also stands in the grand historic tradition. Here are the dramatic renderings of light and shade that define and contour the Antarctic, beautifully rendered to shimmer off the page; and here are the portraits of the crews, better clothed than their predecessors, better equipped, but still unmistakably "expeditionary". Here also are images that the old camera hands of the Heroic Age would have gaped to see – Antarctica from the air. This is a wonderful book, and will be valued by enthusiasts of expeditionary history and Antarctica, and all who are moved by sublime glimpses of the earth's far away places.

Caroline Alexander

Caroline Alexander is the author of the international best sellers *The Endurance: Shackleton's Legendary Antarctic Expedition* and *The Bounty: The True Story of the Mutiny on the Bounty*. Her latest book is *The War That Killed Achilles: The True Story of Homer's Iliad and the Trojan War*. A Contributing Writer for *National Geographic Magazine*, Alexander has also written for the *New Yorker* and *Smithsonian* among other publications.

Previous page:

"Winter Quarters Bay" at the tip of Hut Point Peninsula on Ross Island, the southernmost harbor in the Southern Ocean. Robert Scott's Discovery, *with Shackleton aboard as an officer, moored here in early 1902 and was frozen in for two years. The expedition's chief scientist described it as "the most perfect little natural harbor imaginable."*

◄ *A skua gull circles over the ice of McMurdo Sound. Penguins, seals, and skuas are the only obvious forms of life here that utilize the land and surfaces of the ice. Black Island is in the background, and members of a Weddell seal colony are visible on the ice.*

THE ANTARCTIC HAS A WAY of making exclamation marks in a fellow's life narrative. One summer I was National Science Foundation representative at Palmer Station. The Coast Guard icebreaker Burton Island arrived from McMurdo. Joe Warburton, an amiable atmospheric scientist from the Desert Research Institute in Reno, Nevada, got off, opened two large, black suitcases, and set up an antenna about 4 feet long on the rocky yard between the galley-lab building and the harbor. He aimed it vaguely north and said that ought to be about right. While the two of us stood in a damp maritime breeze, Joe casually dialed Foundation headquarters in Washington, D.C., and handed me something new to Palmer Station: a telephone. I spoke with my colleague Albert P. (Buzz) Betzel as if sitting in the next office. The conversation, on 2 February 1977, was Palmer's first satellite phone call (it used NASA's ATS-3) — an unexpected achievement at our little outpost. Thirty-three years later, the memory is indelible.

Scientists, teachers, diesel mechanics, military officers, doctors, sailors, even tourists are knocked off center by the ice continent's huge scale and minimalist landscape. For years or even lifetimes after, they talk at parties, give slide shows, visit classrooms, write articles, set up web sites, wake up from dreams. A few are moved to write books, typically their first or only: Astronomy on Ice, A Year At The Bottom Of The World, Forty Years on Ice, Innocents on Ice, Frigid Mistress.

I'd expected somehow that reporters and photo-journalists, who go everywhere and see everything, normally would finish their Antarctic assignments and not look back. Not Bob McCabe. Bob was in Antarctica as the International Geophysical Year had just ended, when, historian Dian Belanger writes, "an uncommon mix of people, representing cultures, agencies, organizations, and countries from all the inhabited continents, came together to study the last continent and then to reserve it as a continuing haven for science and peace." All twelve of the Antarctic IGY nations saw the huge potential of discoveries to be made and decided to stay. Bob was there to witness the beginning of the decades-long replacement of temporary camps with facilities that would support the science needed to figure out the ice continent and its complex interplay with global processes.

Fifty years later, scientists and governments have just concluded the 2007-2009 International Polar Year, the fourth such, IGY having been the third. The science has matured, and the pioneering has morphed into a sophisticated and even urgent push for answers to uncomfortable questions about the future of humanity. The number of nations doing research there has more than doubled, to twenty-nine.

We've figured out how to make life in Antarctica safer and more routine, at least much of the time. "I hope my season will be boring," a scientist told me, because then she'd have her data, get her research paper published, and maybe get another National Science Foundation grant to finish solving her part of the Antarctic puzzle and put food on the table back home.

An amazing amount has been learned in the last half century. Stratospheric chemists discovered the ozone hole and realized that anyone who used a refrigerator was part of the blame for it. Decades ago scientists had told us polar regions would warm before the rest of the globe; now it's happening, especially along the Antarctic Peninsula, where whole ice shelves have collapsed and penguin species have shifted south to stay with the ecosystems that let them hang on to life.

New research disciplines have come into play in the Antarctic. More meteorites have been collected on its ice fields than in the rest of the world, giving us a cheap ride into the solar system as chunks of it crash-land here. Science seems on the verge of telling us whether the West Antarctic Ice Sheet is going to melt into the sea, possibly to drown the world's coastal areas that some 700-million now call home. The research station at the South Pole just had its second rebuild since Bob's visit and is now a world-class center for astronomy and astrophysics. The structures he photographed disappeared years ago under the relentlessly accumulating snow and ice.

The Antarctic remains, just beyond camp, as indifferent to our survival as when it tested the explorers, its barren fields ironic testimony to the warmer world's fecundity we'd always expected to support us without limit. The pictures and text in this book — remembered, safeguarded, mulled over by Robert McCabe all these years — are memorials in specific, inimitable detail, transporting us to an earlier and, in some ways, a more optimistic time.

Guy G. Guthridge

Guy G. Guthridge joined the National Science Foundation in 1970 as editor of *Antarctic Journal of the United States*. Later, he ran the N.S.F.'s Polar Information Program, and managed Foundation programs for Antarctic field participation by artists, writers, and photographers. He retired from the Foundation in February 2005 and is working on a book, with Lynn Teo Simarski, about science and society around the Chesapeake Bay.

Boarding the MATS DC-6B at Quonset Point air base.

Cargo for the Antarctic bases being loaded at Quonset Point.

FOUR WEEKS AGO the vast continent which covers the south polar regions of our planet was as remote to my life as the moon. But within three or four days I will be on the ice on McMurdo Sound, and a short time later, at the Pole.

I left New York on Thursday, October 29, 1959 for Washington. The three preceding weeks had been hectic, but now I was in a taxicab on the way to LaGuardia Airport. The little worries about shots and visas and camera equipment were behind me. As we crossed the 59th Street Bridge to Queens, I looked back at the lights of midtown Manhattan and thought what a great contrast there was between this great island city and the vast frozen wastes of Antarctica. I wondered which condition was more fantastic by nature's standards: a great uninhabited continent or a tiny island packed with several million people. Both seemed to be extremes.

At precisely 8:30 Friday morning, our four-motored DC-6B, a Military Air Transport Service (MATS) plane operated by a Navy crew, lifted off the runway at Andrews Air Force Base, Washington. Our first stop was the Quonset Point Base in Rhode Island, where we picked up two more passengers and some cargo destined for McMurdo Sound.

During the last few weeks, and even more so during the last few hours, the Antarctic has been becoming for me an increasingly vivid reality of our world. Even during the weeks in which I was preparing for this trip, it was somehow impossible to really believe that I was going to the Antarctic. Yesterday, as we crossed Pennsylvania, Ohio, Indiana and finally crossed over the Rockies and dropped down into Travis, it was still hard to believe. Today, though, it is different. We have now left behind our continent. In front of us lie thousands of miles of ocean. Somehow today our destination seems clear and inexorable.

Walt Selig and Tom Jones

Bob Williams

THERE ARE TWENTY-FOUR OF US on this flight who are going down to the ice. The largest number are scientific personnel, but there are also six representatives of the press, an Army General, a Florida oilman, a Rhode Island Probate Judge, and an Army Captain who has spent the past few years in Greenland. Friendships have formed fast, and barriers, which in other circumstances might have held up strongly, have been quickly broken by the uniting force of the great adventure upon which we are all embarked. With us is Tom Jones, the director of U.S. scientific research in the Antarctic. He and Admiral David Tyree together hold responsibility for the success of our efforts on the polar continent. Dr. Jones has with him a party of twelve scientists in many different fields. He intends to show them what his people are doing, and at the same time, hopes to get from the group new ideas and points of view about Antarctic research.

From time to time a small group gathers in one part of the airplane – perhaps they are holding a map in front of them, or maybe they are discussing the habits of the killer whales and the sea leopard. The names of bases and glaciers and mountain ranges are becoming more and more familiar to us: McMurdo, Hallett, Scott, Little America, Byrd, Marble Point. Some of the problems of scientific research and some of the problems of just plain existing on an empty frozen continent are becoming vivid.

Most of us are amazed at what has been done in Antarctica by Amundsen, Shackleton, Scott, by Byrd, by Dufek, and many others, but we are also amazed at how much remains to be done and how little is really known about the continent and its mysteries. The aurora has not been fully explained yet, nor has the relationship between the earth's spin poles, its magnetic poles and its geomagnetic poles. Only ten percent of the Antarctic continent has been adequately mapped. Little is known of the continent's geologic mysteries; glacial movements remain, for the most part, uncharted; the habits of Antarctica's animal life are still largely unknown: the killer whales, the penguins, the seals, and others.

Lili of Lili's Leis

Self Portrait. Diamond Head is the backdrop.

Stopover in Hawaii

I T WAS RAINING LIGHTLY LAST NIGHT when our plane pulled up to the MATS Terminal at Hickam Field. After we stepped out of the plane, it took no more than thirty seconds to realize that our fiftieth state is one of the great ones. (Hawaii became a state just three months ago.) There was nothing specific to say this with the possible exception of the sight of Erwin Chernick, the young Providence judge, walking away from the plane with a lei around his neck. For the most part it was simply the atmosphere.

Here at Hickam most of the Deep Freeze press corps (Bob Williams of the *Hartford Courant*; Larry Burrell of KBIG in Hollywood; Gordon White of the *Chicago American*; Dan Hoyt of the *Washington Daily News*; and Robert McCabe) got a special reception: drinks at the Officers' Club and dinner at the Beachcomber Restaurant.

Departure from Hickam

S UNDAY NIGHT, NOVEMBER 1. I am standing at the fence at Hickam AFB. Final preparations are being made on our plane, which is directly in front of me. The sun has already set; it is an overcast evening; in the distance the mountain peaks are cloud-covered.

We are now at the end of Hickam's runway. The time is 18:25; the flight from here to Canton Island is eight hours. There we will re-fuel and leave after an hour and a half or so for Nandi in the Fijis. It is a little sad leaving Honolulu after such a short stay, and we are looking forward to our arrival here again in two weeks.

Our plane is now airborne. To the west faint tinges of red; below us the lights of Honolulu. We have now turned toward the southwest and are climbing into the third leg of our flight to the Pole.

WE ARE NOW SIXTEEN HOURS out of Honolulu, 10,000 feet over the hazy and hot South Pacific. We are expected to arrive in Christchurch in approximately five and a half hours. The flight has been uninterrupted, except for a two hour re-fueling stop early this morning on Canton Island. Throughout our stay it was pitch dark — the blackness broken only by a flashing white and green beacon, the airport terminal lights, and the runway lights. It is a tiny island about eight square miles in area with no point more than 20 feet above sea level. It consists of a pork chop shaped ring of land surrounding a clear lagoon. There are about 300 people living on Canton now. They include British and U.S. government officials, and representatives of Pan American, Qantas, and the Standard Oil Company of California.

This is one of the few places in the world where you can see post offices of two countries side by side competing for mail. This, incredibly enough, is the result of the 1937 eclipse of the sun. At that time, it was selected by both American and British astronomers for ideal viewing of the total eclipse. Subsequently, negotiations were completed which put the island under joint American and British control for fifty years. During the Second World War, a garrison of approximately 1,000 men was stationed on the island and a national anthem was "adopted." It is sung to the tune of the Marine Corps hymn. It goes:

From the harbor's coral entrance
To the palm tree by the pass
You can take this little island and - - - - -

Since the jets went into operation on South Pacific runs, the island has become increasingly lonely. An average of one plane a day stops there. Every four months or so a tanker calls, and occasionally other ships stop. The island's name comes from the New Bedford whaling ship, Canton, which was wrecked there in 1854. The crew took the life boats and after 49 days managed to reach Guam, which is due south, 900 miles away. Canton is a little more than half way between New York and McMurdo Sound. Within the past few hours, we have crossed the equator and the International Date Line. At Canton, we were all unwilling and unwitting buyers of box lunches. My inventory of these little mysterious boxes with their many surprises now stands at three. Box lunches during the course of our trip have either been in too short or too great supply, and have become a standing joke among the passengers.

JUST LANDED at Christchurch International Airport. We leave tomorrow by Super Constellation for McMurdo. The flight is about ten hours down. Arrival at McMurdo is estimated for 18:00 tomorrow. We are now in an auditorium near the airport for a demonstration of survival gear and a briefing on our flight tomorrow morning.

Briefing for the flight to Antarctica:

"Cruising altitude will be 12,000 feet. We will start at 10 or 11 depending on weather conditions en route. We may climb to 12,000 or 14,000 feet to burn off a little fuel to be lighter for the ice runway landing. May go to 17,000 or 18,000 to avoid mountains. En route we will pass 40 miles from Camel Island, and over the destroyer escort Petersen.

"We will be making hourly position reports and later half hourly reports. If the weather looks bad on the way down and we have not reached the halfway point, we may turn around. It is 2,160 miles from Christchurch to McMurdo.

"Aircraft dress suggestions: olive drab trousers and shirt over long underwear. Carry rest of gear. Put on waffle weave shirt and trousers and thermal boots for survival purposes. The cabin will be gradually cooled as we approach. Clothes should be put on progressively as cabin cools.

"There is survival gear for each man aboard: a Mae West, a survival suit, rations, sleds. The life vest has two packages of dye marker, a flashlight, shark chaser (which chases sharks and attracts barracuda) a whistle, and a helicopter hoist. The Mae West goes over all clothing and the survival suit. Survival suits come in one size: extra large. You get into them through the neck. When you go into the water with a survival suit on, go in feet first. If you go in head first, the air is trapped in the feet, and it is almost impossible to right yourself, head up, in the water.

"There is a good Sea Air Rescue program here. The SAR crew will be on the alert tomorrow morning. They are equipped with 20 man rafts. They drop two rafts connected by a line, which drift down wind to those in the sea."

The journalists outside the King George. Author is clutching his thermal boots.

W E ARE SPENDING TONIGHT at the extraordinary King George Hotel, owned and operated by one Mrs. Baily, who serves as chambermaid, cook, room clerk and bartender. The atmosphere of the hotel is more like a private home than a hotel. We paid $4.20 for a room, dinner, and breakfast this morning.

Last night two Christchurch butchers joined us for drinks before dinner. They were dressed in a dignified Ivy League style and spoke in what impressed us as cultured tones. It's spring here, and after dinner I strolled through the town. Christchurch is very quiet at night. Couples and pairs of girls occasionally are seen walking along the main shopping street looking at lighted shop windows. But there's very little open in the way of restaurants and bars. The pubs close at 6 o'clock and after that one can gain admission only through membership, which, I discovered later, is extraordinarily easy to come by.

We have found New Zealanders to be a friendly informal people. Christchurch is a town of 200,000 or one tenth of the population of the entire country. It has few traffic lights and no traffic problems. The import duty on automobiles is virtually prohibitive, bringing the price on a new Chevrolet, for example, to about $5,000.00 — a fortune in New Zealand. Many people ride bicycles and in the morning one sees school children distinctively dressed in the costume of their particular college or school, and class, riding along in groups. New Zealanders have become increasingly aware of the Antarctic in the last few years, especially in the Christchurch area, which is the base of U.S. Antarctic operations. But it is still a wild distant place in the minds of most.

Last night upon our arrival in Christchurch we were issued our Antarctic clothing, including heavy rubber thermal boots, long underwear, woolen sweater, jacket liner, jacket, woolen pants, wool and nylon outer pants, heavy gloves with liners, a hood and cap, sun glasses, goggles, and socks. We donned part of the gear this morning before we left our hotel. The remainder we will put on piece by piece in the airplane as we approach McMurdo Sound. The pilot has told us that he will slowly decrease the cabin temperature so that we will be prepared when the door opens. The clothing we have been issued and the preparations we have made in the last 12 or 15 hours paint a picture of Antarctica in themselves. It becomes quite clear that man's foothold on the continent is tenuous at best.

Preparing to board the Super Constellation at Christchurch.

OUR SUPER CONSTELLATION has just taken off from the airport at Christchurch. We are now climbing to 10,000 feet and will proceed down the coastline of New Zealand's Southern Island to Dunedin. From there we will turn off to McMurdo on a course due south. On our right we have a lovely view of the Alps of southern New Zealand with the Canterbury Plain in front of them. Behind us on the runway as we take off is a specially equipped SAR DC-4 that will follow us into the air and will escort us to the point of no return.

It is now 10:50. We are leaving Dunedin and heading across the open sea toward McMurdo. The pilot has just given us the weather report for McMurdo: high clouds and blowing snow with winds from 25 to 30 miles an hour. Visibility is about 3 miles.

There are about 50 men aboard the aircraft including our group of a dozen scientists, the press group, and the Navy League people. There are also some New Zealanders who are engaged in Antarctic research. I am sitting between Cliff Eliot, a professor of physics at Canterbury University in Christchurch, and Walt Selig of the U.S. Coast and Geodetic Survey, a mapping expert.

The Constellation's interior: life preservers and sledges at the ready.

THE CONSTELLATION is uniquely equipped in the interior. The seats, as in all military planes, are facing the rear. Over the back of each seat is a Mae West, fully equipped with light signals, shark chaser, etc. In racks on the side of the plane above the passengers are survival suits in yellow bags and on each side of the craft are a sledge and skis.

The pilot has told us that we should expect to see pack ice approximately 800 miles off the coast of the Antarctic continent. 360 miles before we reach McMurdo Sound we will pass over the Hallett Base, jointly operated by the U. S. and New Zealand.

Walt Selig

THE JOVIALITY OF OUR GROUP, which increased day-by-day and hour-by-hour on our flight from Washington, is for the moment gone. Suddenly there is a seriousness in the air. The plane has now reached 10,000 feet and the "Fasten Seat Belts" sign has been turned off.

The only humorous touch to the flight so far was Bill Beaufort's going up and down the aisle imitating the smile-less flight attendant on the MATS plane. With the grim face of the orderly he was saying "That'll be $1.25 for your box lunches, please".

It is 12:33. We are passing over Campbell Island. It is the first time the crew of this plane has seen the island since they have been flying this route. I have had a talk during the flight with Bill Baker, the navigator. He reports that our Constellation can use only one alternate landing facility on the entire continent – that at Cape Hallett, where the ice runway is ten miles long. The Marble Point runway is now only 1,700 feet and cannot take a Constellation.

It is now 16:05. The "Fasten Seat Belts" sign is on. We had cruised for an hour in pea soup clouds at 9,500 feet and are now trying to climb above the weather so that we can get a position fix. The only means of determining our position here is the sun. There are naturally no stars visible this time of year; the magnetic compass is useless, and we are far beyond the effective range of the McMurdo radio beacon. We passed over the destroyer escort Petersen an hour and a half ago, and are well beyond the halfway point. It is unfortunate that we have heavy cloud cover since we are now in the area of pack ice.

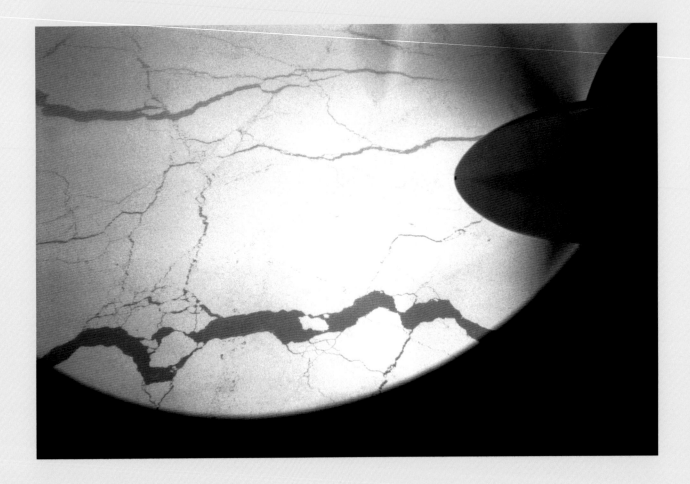

Pack ice with "leads" of the sea.

I T IS 16:32. At 16:15 we reached an altitude of 18,000 feet and as we reached it the sun appeared above us and below us the clouds disappeared, revealing pack ice. We are now passing 20 or 30 miles east of Sturge Island in the Ballenys. Sturge is 170 nautical miles from the Antarctic continent. It is snow covered except for occasional patches of black rock which show at the ice level in two or three spots and here and there on cliff faces.

The pack ice we see below us is eight to ten feet thick. Between the giant floes are leads, or patches of open water, anywhere from a few feet to miles wide. All perspective here is lost in the hazy gray sunlight. In some spots the ice extends miles and miles unbroken. In others it looks as though it has been shattered in thousands of fragments.

It is 17:15 p.m. Forty miles ahead are the snow covered and ice covered hills of Cape Adare, Antarctica, rising out of the ice. It is a beautiful and incredible sight. There is a slight cloud cover beneath us. Often the clouds and the ice are indistinguishable except for the reflections of the sun from the open water.

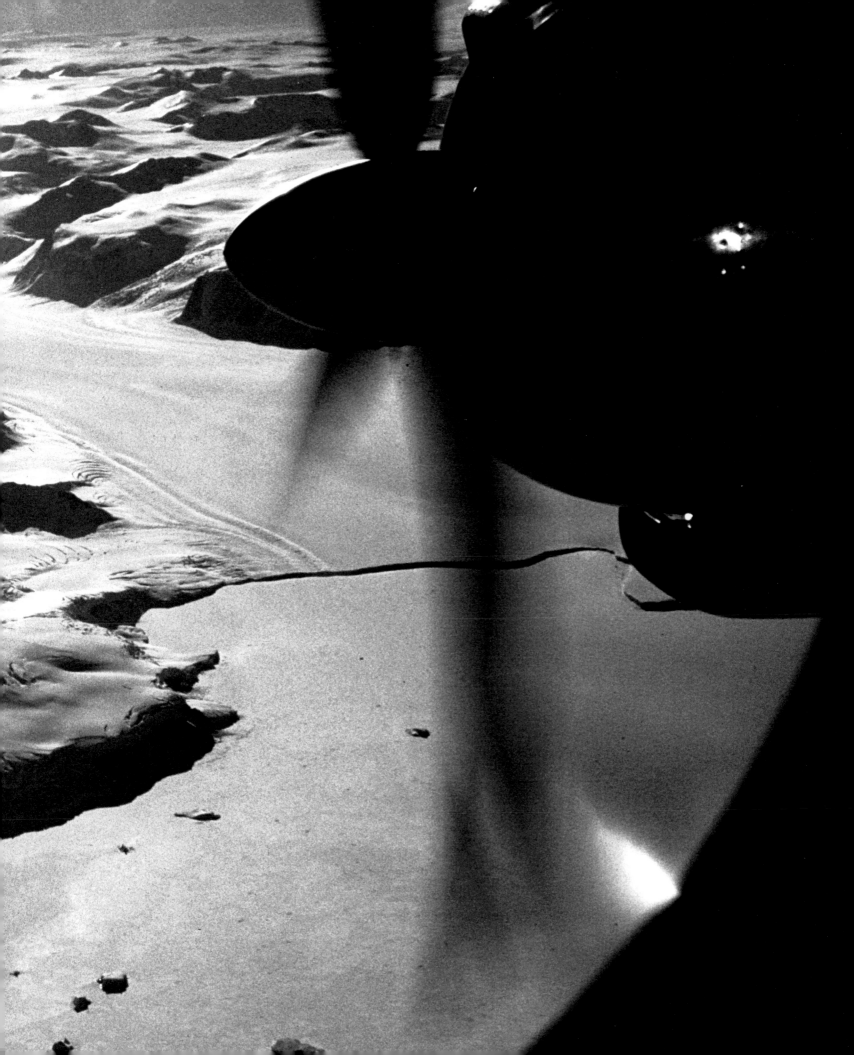

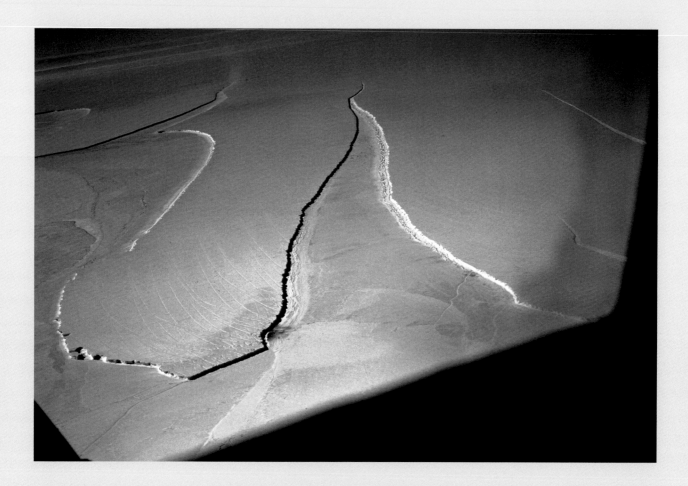

Patterns in the sea ice.

Previous pages: *The Barnett Glacier in coastal northern Victoria Land.*
At the time the photograph was taken the glacier was still unnamed.

I T IS 18:30. We are due in another hour. Since our first visual contact with the continent, the air has been crystal clear. We can see the horizon standing out brilliantly and the sky above us is a very, very deep blue. The pilot says that in all his trips he has never seen such a clear day.

Harry Francis, Dr. Jones' assistant, says that such a day is indeed rare in the Antarctic. The ice of the coast of the continent is now clearly beginning to rot. It is shattered in many areas and there are broad leads. Off our right wing tip now there is a perfect volcanic cone. We are cruising at 17,000 feet.

D URING THE COURSE OF THE LAST HOUR the passengers have been donning their winter equipment and the cabin has been slowly cooling. The cabin looks like a locker room in its activity. I have been taking many photographs of our approach to the coast and our passage along the coast toward McMurdo Sound. I pray that one or two come close to portraying the awesome beauty of this continent, which is as large as the United States and Europe combined. Watching the mountains rise out of the ice here as we pass by the coast it is easy to understand that the Antarctic continent has an average height twice that of any other continent.

During the course of our flight down the coast of Victoria Land from Cape Adare to McMurdo, Walt Selig was busy at one of the port windows on his knees making corrections in the chart. It is amazing to think that despite the fact that this is one of the most known areas of Antarctica the maps are still inaccurate.

It is 19:25. We are now making our descent and are running into a little bit of rough air. A few moments ago we got an excellent view of Mt. Erebus, named after one of Ross' ships, with tiny Beaufort Island in the foreground. We are passing through 2,000 feet. McMurdo is in sight. Ahead the "Fasten Seat Belts" sign has just gone on.

It is 19:31. The flaps are going down. Now on our port side there is a spectacular view of Erebus. It still is very clear and despite the late hour the sun is brilliant and, of course, high in the sky.

Walt Selig, sitting next to me, just said "the Antarctic touch". We are about to make it. We are now perhaps 50 feet off the ice, 25 feet, and we have just about reached the touch down. There! Thump! It was a one bounce landing and very fast on the ice. The propellers are reversed. On the edge of the runway are mounds of ice and drifted snow. The plane has now slowed down. We have reached the Antarctic Continent. It is exactly 19:35.

➤ *An engine of the Constellation is serviced for the return flight to New Zealand.*

Previous pages: *The Super Constellation after landing on the sea ice at McMurdo.*
An old friend of mine, Eugene Armstrong, was a design engineer for Lockheed involved
in the development of the "Connie," so it has always been a special airplane for me.
More than 800 were produced between 1943 and 1958. It was Air Force One
for President Eisenhower, and was operated by many of the major airlines in the world.
Its maximum speed was 375 miles per hour.

"Main Street" at the McMurdo Base and Observation Hill, on whose peak there is a cross in memory of Scott.

THE U.S. STATION AT MCMURDO SOUND is built on Ross Island—a black crater pocked volcanic island. Behind us is Mt. Erebus, a 13,000 foot active volcano, and in front of us across the Sound are Mt. Discovery and a group of other high snow covered peaks which rise vertically out of the frozen sea. All day the sun circles around the base.

McMurdo is in main an operating facility as contrasted with Little America, Byrd, and the Pole Station, which are chiefly scientific in their emphasis. McMurdo is a small city. The current population of over 400 is handled easily and smoothly considering the overwhelming difficulties of transport which face anyone living on this continent.

Admiral David Tyree

"IT'S MIGHTY NICE *to have you down here in Antarctica. I suppose this is the first trip for some of you to land and for many of you it's your first view of this continent. I'm delighted that our weather people have cooperated and that they fixed up some real nice weather. This is probably as fine weather as you will find in the Antarctic. It's a beautiful day out and I just hope it lasts, because it's not typical of what we've had the last month. Later on our weather man will show you the weather picture for the day, and if we can keep these nice clear days, I'm sure you're going to enjoy what you see of the Antarctic. I usually say to people back home and in New Zealand that you just can't describe Antarctica, you have to see it. You can watch colored slides; you can read stories about it; you can see moving pictures; but there's something about the feel of it that you have to get right here on the spot. I hope that all of you will have an opportunity to take some of these Globemaster trips around the continent. And when you do, and get a feel for the vastness of the place, with some of the stupendous scenery, I think you will understand what I mean.*"

NOW AND OVER the next few summer months this base will be at its very busiest. Air activity started here over a month ago on the ice runway. When the weather is good, flying goes on around the clock. There is a constant shuttle of men and material between Christchurch, McMurdo, the Pole, and Byrd station. Material destined for the Pole and Byrd must be trans-shipped here. The Air Force has so far been doing the dropping to Byrd and the Pole. They have almost completed their job and will in a few days be flying back to the States with their Globemasters. After that the Navy will take over and landings at the Pole will start.

Within a month or so the ice runway at McMurdo will have melted beyond use for the remainder of the summer. Then there will be a shift from wheels to skis and a new runway on more permanent ice will be established. Aerial photographs of possible sites for such a runway were just completed yesterday. Soon, too, the first ice breakers will be arriving and soon after them tankers, cargo ships, and transports with replacements.

The society here at McMurdo is rather unique. Everyone has his job to do and there is a great deal of interdependence. The cooks, the mechanics, the pilots, the parachute riggers, the vehicle drivers, the radio men, the photographers all have their jobs and all are important to the life, safety, and success of the others. It is a real spectacle and one worth observing closely - how cooperation increases as people have to rely on one another.

The airport shuttle on the ice runway. In the background is the McMurdo based fleet of De Havilland U-1A Otters. These were retired from Antarctic service in 1966, replaced by a twin engine version. At least 7 of these were lost in Antarctic service, including one that blew away from the base in Little America. It had a 600 H.P. Pratt & Whitney engine and could take off in a few hundred feet. It was at home on floats, skis, amphibious floats, and wheels. In 1958 an Otter made the first non-stop crossing of the Antarctic continent in a single engine aircraft. It took 11 hours. Mt. Discovery is in the background.

Larry Burrell in front of the VXE-6 ready room at McMurdo's Williams Air Terminal on the ice.

A shuttle from the air field.

Antarctic destinations

A McMurdo denizen

A visitor sketches scenes from the McMurdo base.

The author on his front porch.

Hut Point on a clear Antarctic day, with the Transantarctic Mountains in the distance, some 35 miles from the camera.

O UR ARRIVAL HERE was actually somewhat comic. We had prepared for many hours our clothing and had struggled to put on boots and pants, shirts, sweaters, and jackets, and hoods and caps, only to find out that while it was not balmy when we got out of the airplane it was actually not much colder than waiting for a New York, New Haven, and Hartford train in the New York suburbs on a winter morning. We had prepared for the worst, but had gotten the best. Only a few days before us a group of correspondents had arrived in a raging blizzard. We have been here 48 hours and the sun has not disappeared once. What good fortune!

It is strange living in this world of constant sunlight. We who come from the east normally associate cold with darkness. To have 24 hours of sunlight and blue sky and cold is a wonderful thing. Meals are served from five to seven, a.m. and p.m.; from eleven to one, a.m. and p.m. One can live on any cycle he wishes, as the sun circles over Erebus, over Crater Hill, over Mt. Discovery and over Observation Hill, and over the ridge behind the camp. This morning at 1:30, I strolled around the camp taking photographs. This is a place where a photographer can never sleep in peace.

Scientist "fishing" for specimens through a seal hole. The base of Observation Hill is on the left.

OUR FIRST DAY HERE was spent with a morning briefing by Admiral Tyree and some of his associates, and an afternoon trip to the ice. There we saw several seals. They are an unusual animal, who neither seem to mind nor pay attention to human beings. True, when you come within three or four feet to take a photograph, they may open their mouth with a toothy and at first frightening gesture, but for the most part they spend their time moaning and groaning, rolling around on the ice like a fish out of water, making noises which seem to convey a certain sense of being mistreated. A seal can make and hold a single note for what seems like an indefinite period. You hear it in the distance and it sounds like a railroad train with its whistle stuck at a nearby station. It is easy to understand why the fur seals are practically extinct. Seal hunting, which is presently carried out on a limited scale for the purpose of feeding the huskies, consists of walking up to a seal with a shotgun and shooting it point blank. [Today seal hunting is strictly prohibited.]

While on the ice, I watched two "fishermen" at work through an enlarged seal hole. Seals spend their winters in water keeping warm, but to breathe must poke their heads out of water. To accomplish this, they have to keep a hole open, or if they intend to move somewhere, must keep a series of holes open spaced at intervals along the route. Two American scientists were using this seal hole to fish with a metal net and a long streamer net designed to catch plankton. In the wire net were two fish, each about four inches long and of a light brown color. They had large heads and a body, which tapered to a point at the tail. The fishermen encountered great difficulty with their plankton net. Whenever they tried to raise it above the water level – the sea water temperature being about 29 degrees – into the air, it would immediately freeze, making it impossible to extricate the plankton.

➤ *Seal mother and pup with their breathing hole,*
which must be continuously kept open.

Weddell seals: mother and pup.

Greeting a seal pup.

A husky sled dog

➤ *A stroll to Hut Point.*

Ross Island vista.

A Navy vessel locked in the ice is utilized for fuel storage.

SACRED TO THE MEMORY OF
GEORGE T. VINCE
AB.RN
OF THE
"DISCOVERY"
WHO WAS DROWNED NEAR THIS SPOT
MARCH 11TH, 1902

Hut Point

Scott's Discovery Hut was prefabricated in Australia. Many hours were spent digging through
the permafrost for the foundations, but by early March, 1902 it was fully erected.
The hut was utilized twice by Scott-led expeditions, and twice by Shackleton expeditions.

Hiking on Ross Island. Mt. Erebus, one of two active volcanoes in the Antarctic, is in the background.

The radio room at McMurdo, housed in a Quonset hut.

THERE ARE SOME VERY AGREEABLE ASPECTS to life on Ross Island. Meals are excellent and there is an ample supply of beer and movies, mostly westerns. Besides, the company includes a number of very good storytellers who apparently do not run out of yarns during the long winter night. Only the beer offers difficulties. Antarctica's beer is either warm or frozen. So far I have not found any in between. When the beer is warm you either drink it, happy that it is not frozen, or put it in the snow to cool it off. If the beer is frozen, one simply drinks the alcohol off the top and discards the ice; it is a very potent way of taking one's beer.

One of the intriguing facilities here is the ham radio station, which allows one to telephone anyone in the States for a very minimal price. The ham shack here contacts a station in or near the destination of the call and the ham at the stateside end puts in a phone call to the callee. These calls are placed collect and the only charge is for the telephone service from the ham to the recipient. There are some unsung heroes among the hams who receive these calls. One of them is a young man by the name of Jules Madley who lives in Clark, New Jersey, and apparently stays up all night every night to complete calls from the Antarctic to the eastern U.S. It was he who completed the call that I made home two or three days ago. (I later met Jules in a Christchurch hotel, on his way to the Antarctic as a special guest of the Navy.) This radio station is a great morale booster and a great thrill to use.

After trying for many hours to adjust myself to a day and night schedule I have given up. There is no such thing as day or night in the Antarctic summer. The Navy serves meals here from five to seven, a.m. and p.m., and eleven to one, a.m. and p.m. You just go to bed when you are tired and get up either when you have had enough sleep or are hungry.

THE McMURDO AIR FACILITY AND BASE have a very beautiful setting which offers fresh vistas at every hour of the day as the sun moves around. To the west is a range of 12,000 foot mountains, which include the extinct volcanic peak Mt. Discovery. To the southeast is Observation Hill, a 900 foot volcanic hill. To the north is Mount Erebus, one of two active volcanoes in the Antarctic. Erebus is not visible from the base but it can be seen beautifully from the air strip on the ice. To the northeast is Crater Hill, a 400 foot extinct volcano with twin craters. The day before yesterday, I climbed Observation Hill over a combination of ice and loose volcanic rock in the company of Harry Francis, Dr. Wolfe, and Dr. Frederick Baker. At the peak there is a cross in memory of Robert Falcon Scott, whose hut is clearly visible from the peak.

The McMurdo base is full of little touches which make everyone's life happier. For example, on the road from the airstrip to the base, a distance of four and a half miles, there are Burma Shave signs and U.S. route number signs. Most of McMurdo's huts have colorful names. There is the Ross Hilton for visiting dignitaries, the Beverly Hilton for Officers, the Wheel House, the McMurdo Heights Resort, and the Texas Immigration Office, which houses the hospital.

There is a notable discrepancy between the outlook of the men who are here for just a short time, flying cargo into the Pole or attending to other summer jobs, and the men who will winter over. Among the summer transients there is a certain amount of complaining about having to live at this lonely, desolate spot. Among the wintering party, however, there is obvious zest and enthusiasm for the job. Two different breeds of cats.

➤ *A view from Observation Hill toward Hut Point and Winter Quarters Bay, showing the McMurdo Base.*

L AST NIGHT I MET A PENGUIN. It was standing with great dignity and formality in the bedroom of a Navy officer. It was an Emperor penguin and looked as though it was waiting for the Admiral to come and inspect his quarters. It was a young Emperor and stood under three feet tall. He was a friendly bird with a great deal of curiosity. We put him on a bar to take photographs, and when we were finished he stood there looking around as though he wanted more photos taken.

His coloring was more brilliant than I had expected. Besides the black and white he had areas of bright orange at the side of his head. From time to time he would struggle, but when we took him outside he just walked a couple of yards away and stood there, still puzzled I suppose by the antics of the Antarctic visitors. Then finally he walked off by himself toward the frozen sea.

Visiting Emperor

The visiting Emperor penguin with a member of the McMurdo base team.

Returning to the sea ice.

A view of pressure ice, en route to the Scott Base in a Snocat.

Y ESTERDAY I WENT TO THE SCOTT BASE of New Zealand. It is a much smaller base than ours and is designed only for scientific research and not for supply purposes like McMurdo. The New Zealand base is graced by such luxuries as Antarctica's only bathtub. From the campsite there is a spectacular view of pressure ice where the Ross Ice Shelf meets McMurdo Sound.

The Scott Base is the capital of what New Zealanders refer to as the Ross Dependency. They consider it a territory of New Zealand. Among other things it has its own commemorative postage stamps. The Scott base is only two miles from the U.S. base at McMurdo. It is in effect just over the hill, on the other side of the peninsula, which at that point is very narrow.

Paul W. Haiser, an American auroral physicist who wintered over at Scott Base.

Scott Base

Pressure ice near the Scott Base.
Castle Rock is at the left,
and Mt. Erebus in the center.

WE WERE INVITED ON A HELICOPTER TRIP to see two Antarctic "archaeological" sites: Scott's hut on Cape Evans, and Shackleton's hut at Cape Royds. The visit to Cape Royds also included a look at the Adelie penguin rookery there. These sites are within 20 miles as the crow flies of our base here at McMurdo. Shackleton had selected Cape Royds for a base in 1907 when pack ice prevented him from reaching McMurdo. From this spot Shackleton launched an expedition to the Pole utilizing the Beardmore Glacier. He came within 97 miles of the Pole before deciding to turn back. The hut includes stables for ponies, and kennels for the huskies.

➤ *Wave off from McMurdo.*

The McMurdo heliport at the foot of Observation Hill.

Aboard a Navy helicopter en route to Cape Evans and Cape Royds.

A perfectly preserved wooden crate for provisions from the 1907 British expedition.

The kitchen of Shackleton's Cape Royds hut.

*Ernest Shackleton's hut at Cape Royds, some 20 miles north of the McMurdo Base.
The hut was erected in February 1908 and served as the primary base for Shackleton's
failed attempt to reach the Pole in 1909. He had wanted to base at McMurdo but ice
prevented his ship from making it to Winter Quarters Bay.*

➤ *At Cape Royds: a discarded Colman's mustard tin.
The Adelie penguin colony is in the background.*

At Cape Royds

Adelie penguins at the Cape Royds rookery.

Scott's Hut at Cape Evans on Ross Island. This hut served as the primary base for Scott's second expedition to Antarctica, the Terra Nova *expedition of 1910-1913. It was the base for Scott's ill-fated journey to the South Pole.*

Scott described it in the following terms:

The hut is becoming the most comfortable dwelling-place imaginable. We have made unto ourselves a truly seductive home, within the walls of which peace, quiet, and comfort reign supreme. Such a noble dwelling transcends the word "hut," and we pause to give it a more fitting title only from lack of the appropriate suggestion. What shall we call it?

The word "hut" is misleading. Our residence is really a house of considerable size, in every respect the finest that has ever been erected in the Polar regions; 50 ft. long by 25 wide and 9 ft. to the eaves. If you can picture our house nestling below this small hill on a long stretch of black sand, with many tons of provision cases ranged in neat blocks in front of it and the sea lapping the ice foot below, you will have some idea of our immediate vicinity.

As for our wider surroundings it would be difficult to describe their beauty in sufficiently glowing terms. Cape Evans is one of the many spurs of Erebus and the one that stands closest under the mountain, so that always towering above us we have the grand snowy peak with its smoking summit. North and south of us are deep bays, beyond which great glaciers come rippling over the lower slopes to thrust high blue-walled snouts into the sea. The sea is blue before us, dotted with shining bergs or ice floes, whilst far over the Sound, yet so bold and magnificent as to appear near, stand the beautiful Western Mountains with their numerous lofty peaks, their deep glacial valley and clear cut scarps, a vision of mountain scenery that can have few rivals.

Ponting is the most delighted of men; he declares this is the most beautiful spot he has ever seen and spends all day and most of the night in what he calls "gathering it in" with camera and cinematograph. [Herbert G. Ponting, the great Antarctic photographer.]

A view north from the beach at Cape Evans: the ice cliff in the distance is the terminus of the Barne Glacier.

A helicopter view of R4Ds on the ice runway.

The western slope of Mt. Bird
on the northern coast of Ross Island.
Beaufort Island is in the distance.

Mt. Lister, Mt. Hooker and Mt. Roper,
with the Koettlitz Glacier
in the foreground.

YESTERDAY WE WENT FOR A FLIGHT around the area in an old R4D. The R4D was the Navy version of the Douglas DC-3. We made a circle around Ross Island and Mt. Erebus and then headed west across the Sound toward Marble Point. We flew up Taylor Glacier, with a breathtaking series of panoramas up and down the immense river of ice.

The Skelton and Baronick glaciers

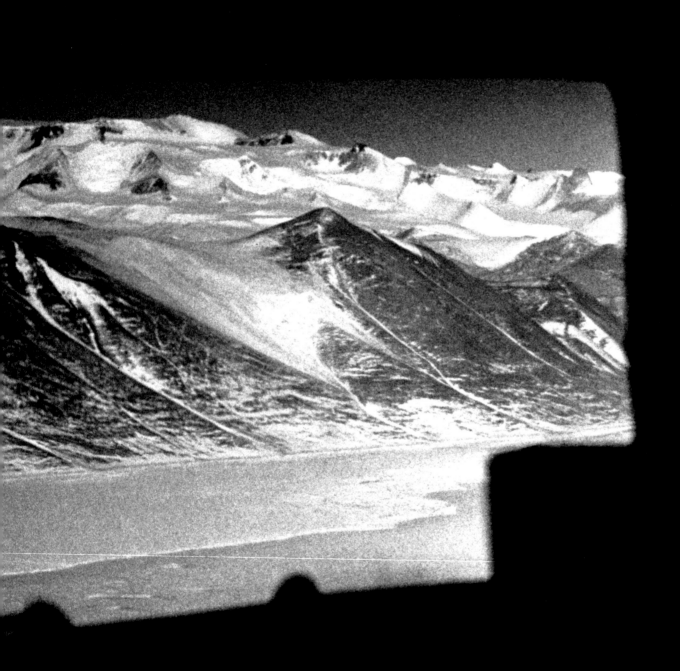

Map of aerial way points in the Antarctic.

Previous pages: *The Ferrar Glacier where it meets the Ross Ice Shelf, near Ross Island.*
The transition from glacier to sea ice is visible in the foreground.

McMurdo air traffic controller.

I AM SPEAKING FROM THE CARGO HOLD of a C-124 Globemaster en route to the South Pole. It is Sunday, November 9. We took off 40 minutes ago. Within four hours we should be over the Pole and dropping our cargo to the men stationed there.

The hold of a Globemaster looks much like a section of a subway tunnel. It is an immense airplane. The plane can be converted to passenger use by putting in a second deck in the cargo hold. We have a rather small load today, consisting of oxygen and JATO bottles and other miscellaneous gear. The JATO (Jet Assisted Take Off) bottles are needed frequently for take offs at the Pole's high altitude. The cabin of this aircraft is not pressurized and as we climb over the mountains to the polar plateau we have been told to expect moments of heavy breathing if we move around the aircraft.

➤ *Preparation for the polar flight. The C-124 Globemaster was developed by Douglas Aircraft and produced between 1950 and 1955. The plane had giant clamshell doors to facilitate loading, as well as a ramp. It could carry 68,000 pounds of cargo, powered by four 3,800 H.P. Pratt & Whitney piston engines. It was the first U.S. aircraft that could accommodate a fully assembled bulldozer or tank.*

Previous pages: *The Taylor Glacier looking east. Lake Bonney is just beyond the end of the glacier. Mt. Erebus on Ross Island is in the distance.*

The Globemaster prior to departure for the Pole. Mt. Erebus is in the background.

The Globemaster's wingtip pods contained combustion heaters for the cabin and for the de-icing system.

The giant "thimble" on the nose housed the Globemaster's weather radar equipment.

The Beardmore Glacier, named for the Glasgow steel magnate who sponsored Shackleton's 1907 expedition.

The Supporters Range, en route to the Pole.

I AM SITTING ON A PARACHUTE with my back leaning against one of the pieces of cargo which we will drop at the Pole. (But I am too close to the starboard engines so I am going to move to another part of the aircraft to see if it is any easier to record.)

We are over the Ross Ice Shelf. For miles and miles around us there is nothing but flat unbroken ice. The sky now is a brilliant clear blue, and if one looks far into the distance perhaps to 75 or 100 miles it is possible to see the mountains of the continent.

Approaching the polar plateau.

I T IS NOW 12:25, and we have just completed the flight up the spectacular Beardmore Glacier to the Polar Plateau. We are cruising at an altitude of 12,000 feet and are due over the Pole in one hour. As far as the eye can see around us there is nothing but ice—grooved, wind-swept and polished.

I am sitting in the upper level of our C-124 Globemaster. Here there is the cockpit, the engineer's and navigator's desks, three beds, and a kitchenette. Luncheon is now being served and the pilot has just opened an enormous can of corned beef. As an appetizer, I had sardines and liverwurst.

The pilot of this aircraft is Carl Kimble of Greenville, South Carolina. Most of the crew live in Greenville and are stationed at Donaldson Air Force Base. I am sitting now with Captain Kimble, and he is giving us an idea of how the drop will be conducted. We are expected to arrive over the Pole in exactly one hour, at 13:40. We will first fly over the South Pole Station, and then circle and make a drop pass. On the first pass, we will drop seven bundles. There will then be a lapse of approximately 12 minutes as preparations are made for the second drop pass. On the second pass, we will drop nine bundles. We will fly across the Pole at an altitude of 1,250 feet.

The pilot points to the South Pole.

WE ARE NOW ARRIVING over the South Pole. Our speed has slowed considerably and we are preparing to make a pass before we begin the drop. The South Pole can only be described as an immensely desolate spot surrounded by a desert of ice for hundreds and hundreds of miles in each direction. Our vapor trails leave beautiful shadows on the ice as do the high clouds which we have today.

We are now starting our drop run. I am listening over the intercom. The buzzer has just gone off to signal the drop. The plane has given several distinct lurches and we are now past the Pole.

*Circling the Pole, with the shadows of our contrails defining
the Pole on the desolate polar plateau.*

"THIS IS AIRMAN 2ND CLASS WATSON, *the drop master on the aircraft. I come from Tallahassee, Florida, and this is the ninth drop on Operation Deepfreeze Phase 5 for me. This is the ninth one I have been the drop master on and we are going to make this one at approximately 1200 feet and we will make two passes. The first pass we will drop seven containers each weighing approximately 2,000 pounds. On the second pass, we will drop nine containers of the same weight. Everything seems to be going all right so far on this and we should get 100% but in just a few minutes we will know. We have just completed the first pass and we got a message from the ground that all seven parachutes opened and all the bundles landed safely. While preparing for the second pass, we've had a little bit of trouble with one of the parachutes that got entangled with an electrical hoist used for lifting the bundles around in the plane and it's in pretty bad shape and looks like it may not open but we'll know shortly.*

"We're lining up now for the second and final pass and we'll drop the nine containers and just hope that that one parachute opens. The navigator is giving a countdown now and the bundles are away. I don't think the parachute opened and in just a moment we'll have a report from the pilot who'll let me know if it opened or not. The pilot has confirmed one streamer on the second pass. It's believed to be the one that was in such bad condition and, well, it's nothing unusual. This happens every once in a while. It's a pretty expensive loss, but nonetheless there'll be another flight tomorrow and we'll be able to make it up. The reports from the ground say that we got all the bundles in pretty close to the drop zone and they're all recoverable and it looks like it's 100% even."

Preparing for the cargo drop.

A Close Escape

T HE DROP MASTER TOLD ME a harrowing story about Emil Schulthess' flight to the Pole. Schulthess was a great Swiss photographer who published a book of photographs of the Antarctic in 1960. He had been on a previous flight to the Pole and had wanted to photograph in the cargo hold of the Globemaster during the drop. The drop master rigged him up with a harness and showed him where to hook himself to the sides of the hold. During the drop, the drop master saw from the corner of his eye a struggling figure headed for the cargo door. Schulthess had hooked himself to a cargo bundle by mistake and was saved by a quick slash from the drop master's knife, always kept in his boot.

A Penguin Parachutes

A BOUT NINE DAYS AGO Max Watson dropped a penguin at the South Pole. It was the first penguin ever known to have parachuted from an airplane and I want Max to tell about it in his own words:

"The idea of dropping a penguin at the South Pole Station came from a Staff Sergeant Kelly when he found a penguin that was frozen in a scientific hut at McMurdo Sound. He came up with the idea of dropping it so the boys at the South Pole Station could have a mascot, even if it was a frozen penguin. He saw the necessary people to have the penguin given to him, and then he brought it to me for rigging a parachute and setting it up so it could be dropped. Right away I went to work on it, and we put Willie in a box and we sealed him up, packed him all up with some absorbent cotton and tied the box up and then attached a small three foot parachute. The parachute is normally used for extracting a large parachute. The day of the drop came. We all gathered around back by the open door and everybody said their last farewells to old Willie and wished him a good trip down. I connected his line to the aircraft and mailed him out, and the parachute opened and Willie got a safe ride down and the boys at the Pole Station got him, and he was in good condition."

The Liv Base was set up in 1956 on the Liv Glacier. It was designed as a refueling station for the R4Ds, which couldn't make it to the Pole and back on a single tank of fuel.

The Globemaster's shadow on the Liv glacier.

- -

THE RADIO OPERATOR, Roy Stevens, has written a poem commemorating a recent event at the South Pole:

The crew before us did an excellent job
But with the mail situation sure played hob,
43 pounds they dropped and wound up in a hole,
For only one pound belonged to the South Pole.
Air Freight or Postal sure goofed in their zones,
For heard now at Byrd Land are moans and groans.
42 pounds is a great morale booster,
Right now they'd hit the goofer right in the snooster.

This poem commemorates the preceding Globemaster flight to the Pole on which the crew inadvertently dropped mail destined for the Byrd Station. It will be a month or more before a plane can land at the South Pole and pick up the mail for redelivery.

Return to McMurdo

- -

I AM SPEAKING FROM THE EMPTY CARGO HOLD of our Globemaster as it passes over the Ross Ice Shelf. We have completed the lovely and spectacular trip down the Beardmore Glacier, the 40-50 mile wide highway of ice which descends from the 10,000 foot polar plateau to the Ross Ice Shelf. At the foot of the Beardmore, we detoured briefly to fly over the Liv Camp of the U.S. It is a small isolated outpost and not one of our more important bases here in the Antarctic. We circled very low and could clearly see the men.

The cargo hold of the Globemaster after the drop at the Pole.

TODAY I HAVE BEEN AROUND the world five times. The entire trip took little more than thirty minutes. The vehicle of course was a lumbering Globemaster with its flaps down circling precisely at the 1,250 foot level above the ice. Seeing the lonely Polar outpost of the United States is a very thrilling experience. In today's world there is no greater isolation than that experienced by the men who winter at the Pole. They live in a world of 24 hour darkness with temperatures that go down to -102 Fahrenheit. Their base is totally inaccessible: all our modern means of transportation have not yet been able to defeat the Antarctic night. [Author's note: In 2001 a Twin Otter made the first winter flight to the South Pole for a medical evacuation. The temperature on the ground was -68 Celsius or -90.4 Fahrenheit.]

The ice that we flew over today at the Pole at an altitude of 1,250 feet is almost two miles in depth. This is really an incredible thing. Imagine two miles of ice over New York City. The polar plateau, as far as the eye can tell, is a level unbroken expanse of ice. The only markings on the surface are the deep grooves which the wind makes and polishes. At times these look like a canvas from close up with oil paints brushed onto the surface. The only other thing besides the grooves that give the plateau character are the streaks of light and dark created by the cloud shadows on the ice.

The feat of Scott and Amundsen seems more incredible than ever now after our flight over the deep crevasses of the Beardmore Glacier and the ice wasteland of the polar plateau. Our weather today was good, but it is not always so, as Robert Scott and many others have tragically learned.

*The cross on Observation Hill erected in 1912 in memory of Scott
and the members of his expedition who died returning from the Pole.*

ROBERT FALCON SCOTT and his four companions reached the South Pole on January 17, 1912. But they were late. Thirty-five days earlier Roald Amundsen had reached the Pole and planted the Norwegian flag.

Scott and his team did not make it back alive. Two and a half months later, out of food and fuel, they died 11 miles from their next supply depot, trapped in their tent on the Ross Ice Shelf by a howling gale and drifting snow. They had successfully crossed the Polar Plateau and descended the Beardmore Glacier. Their final camp was within 160 miles of Hut Point. On March 29, 1912, Scott made his final journal entry:

> We shall stick it out
> to the end, but we
> are getting weaker of
> course and the end
> cannot be far.
> It seems a pity but
> I do not think I can
> write more—
> R. Scott
>
> Last Entry
> For God's sake look
> after our people

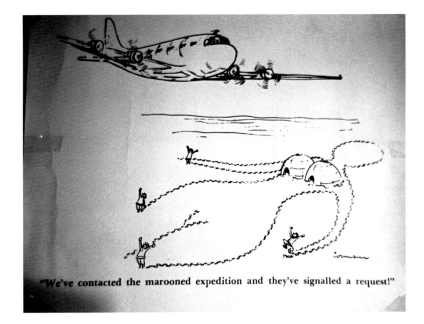

Seen on the wall in the radio shack.

FIFTY YEARS AGO, in the Antarctic summer of 1959, I had the enormous privilege of visiting the Antarctic as a photo journalist. The article I wrote appeared in the New York *Sunday Mirror Magazine* under the title "Around the World in 90 Seconds"—reflecting the headline writer's view of the time a lumbering C-124 Globemaster with its flaps down might take to circle the South Pole.

With the passage of time, coupled with the dramatic changes that have taken place to life in the Antarctic bases, I decided to present additional photographs and text describing my trip to "the ice" in what already appears to be ancient times in the Antarctic. It is hard to believe that more time has passed since my visit than had passed between Amundsen's arrival at the Pole in December 1911 and my trip in November 1959 in the comfort and safety of a Globemaster.

The text is by and large what I dictated to my portable recorder at the time. I have removed some extraneous observations, and have added a few anecdotal and informational items, including the extraordinary story of how the great Swiss photographer Emil Schulthess almost lost his life at the South Pole. I have kept the present tense in the narrative, to give a sense of immediacy, but is certainly not meant to convey the way things are today in the Antarctic.

Many of the things we did or witnessed during our visit are no longer permitted, such as casually hugging penguins or killing seals to feed the huskies. Many steps have been taken to protect the environment and the fauna under the terms of the Antarctic Treaty. Today there are over 100 buildings at McMurdo. Televison and internet are provided by satellite, and there's an ATM, among other amenities.

While new technologies and facilities have made life in the Antarctic easier and more comfortable, it is still a dangerous and inhospitable environment. Many who have served there have lost their lives. And it is to those courageous individuals that this book is dedicated.

Robert A. McCabe
Athens, April, 2010

I am profoundly grateful to Dr. Scott Borg, the division director for Antarctic Sciences of the National Science Foundation, and to Bob Allen and Daniel Secrist, senior cartographers of the United States Geological Survey, for their assistance in providing precise and current names for some important topographical features. And my thanks to Larry Conrad for some detailed identifications. Larry is the author of the remarkable and exhaustive *Bibliography of Antarctic Exploration/ Expedition Accounts from 1768 to 1960.*

I thank Dr. David Harrowfield, geographer and Antarctic historian, not only for his help, but for his passionate interest in preserving the explorers' huts of Ross Island. His histories of the huts are available on the website of the New Zealand Antarctic Heritage Trust and are well worth reading.

Thanks to Gabriel Bauret, Alexis Veroucas, and Anna Pataki for their many valuable contributions to the shaping of this book, as well as to Daniel Ritchie, Randall Warner, and Renee Pappas. And as always my thanks to Sue Medlicott.

My thanks to Vasso Avramopoulou, Chris Simatos and Nikos Vourliotis for their patience and hard work in designing the book. And thanks to George and Sophie Marinos for their excellent prints and scans.

Thanks to Macmillan & Co., Ltd. and to Unilever, to Billy-Ace and Pat McCormick, and my thanks to Guy Guthridge for sharing with us his profound knowledge and love of the Antarctic in his Introduction.

My profound thanks to the Hon. Alexandra Shackleton, President of the James Caird Society, for her help and support, and to Mrs. Pippa Hare, the Secretary of the Society (www.Jamescairdsociety.com). Thanks also to Caroline Alexander, author of the moving bestseller *The Endurance: Shackleton's Legendary Antarctic Expedition,* for reading the manuscript. I thank John Doyle of Crawford Doyle Booksellers in New York for his thoughtful comments and help. Similar thanks go to Catherine Cahill, Sherri Gill, and Ken Siman.

The maps are based on maps produced by the United States Geological Survey. The extraordinary satellite photograph of the Ross Island area is from LIMA-Landsat Image Mosaic of Antarctica. The U.S. Geological Survey (USGS), the British Antarctic Survey (BAS), and the National Aeronautics and Space Administration (NASA), with funding from the National Science Foundation (NSF), created LIMA from more than 1,000 Landsat ETM+ scenes. I appreciate the opportunity to use these remarkable images which convey the reason why the early explorers gravitated to Ross Island and especially Hut Point better than any 10,000 words could.

I am privileged and grateful to again be working with Massimo Tonolli and his team at Trifolio in Verona in the printing of this book. There is no one more skilled in the printing of photographic images.

The endpapers present a map and a satellite photograph of the same small neighborhood in Antarctica. The view includes McMurdo, the largest research station on the continent, located at the tip of Hut Point Peninsula on Ross Island. McMurdo has been operated by the United States since 1956. Its neighbor, Scott Base, is operated by New Zealand. Winter Quarters Bay at Hut Point was the mooring for Scott's vessel *Discovery* in 1901.

Ross Island is roughly 45 miles across. Scott and Shackleton established three bases on the island, each of which has survived. The flat, white areas in the remarkable photograph are the Ross Ice Shelf and other sea ice off the coast of Antarctica. The sea ice just south of Hut Point is used as an airstrip. Also visible are the Erebus Glacier Tongue on Ross Island, and the Koettlitz and Ferrar Glaciers, and the Royal Society Range on the mainland.

The position of the sea ice illustrates why Ross Island was selected by Scott, Shackleton and others as their base, and why Hut Point, at the southern tip of the island, was not the only location utilized: before today's powerful icebreakers, the fine harbor at Hut Point was not always open for business, even at the height of summer.

Scott's ship *Discovery* was frozen in there for two years and had to be blasted out. Subsequent expeditions of both Scott and Shackleton were stalled out by sea ice at Cape Evans and Cape Royds respectively and had to base in those spots rather than Hut Point, which is just 20 miles farther south. The map is based on a map of the United States Geological Survey.

The satellite photograph of the Ross Island area is from LIMA--Landsat Image Mosaic of Antarctica.

THE BOOK

DeepFreeze!

WITH PHOTOGRAPHS BY ROBERT A. McCABE.
PRINTED FROM SCANS BY GEORGE MARINOS
WAS SET IN GARAMOND BY A4 ARTDESIGN
STUDIO IN ATHENS AND PRINTED BY TRIFOLIO
IN VERONA, ITALY ON 150 GR PHOENIXMOTION
XENON IN FEBRUARY 2010, FOR INTERNATIONAL
PHOTOGRAPHY PUBLISHERS LLC. THE BOOK
WAS DESIGNED BY VASSO AVRAMOPOULOU